First Facts

The LIFE and TIMES of the First Americans

by Marissa Kirkman

CAPSTONE PRESS
a capstone imprint

First Facts are published by Capstone Press,
1710 Roe Crest Drive, North Mankato, Minnesota 56003
www.mycapstone.com

Library of Congress Cataloging-in-Publication Data
Names: Kirkman, Marissa, author.
Title: The life and times of the first Americans / by Marissa Kirkman.
Description: North Mankato, Minnesota : First Facts, an imprint of Capstone Press, 2017. | Series: First facts. Life and times | Includes bibliographical references and index. | Audience: K to Grade 3. | Audience: 7 to 9.
Identifiers: LCCN 2016006113 | ISBN 9781515724759 (library binding) | ISBN 9781515724834 (pbk.) | ISBN 9781515724872 (ebook pdf)
Subjects: LCSH: Indians of North America--Juvenile literature.
Classification: LCC E77.4 .K563 2017 | DDC 970.004/97--dc23
LC record available at http://lccn.loc.gov/2016006113

Editorial Credits
Charmaine Whitman, designer; Tracy Cummins, media researcher;
Tori Abraham, production specialist

Image Credits
Bridgeman Images: ©Wood Ronsaville Harlin, Inc. USA/Rob Wood, 7, 13, Peter Newark Western Americana, 17; Capstone Press: Mapping Specialist, 5 Bottom; Getty Images: Hulton Archive, Cover; Granger NYC: 9; North Wind Picture Archives: 1, 5 Top, 15, 19, 21; Shutterstock: Apostrophe, Design Elements, digitalfarmer, 10, Joyce Sherwin, 6, MarclSchauer, 11

Printed in the United States 6578

Table of Contents

Who Were the First Americans? 4
Tribes of the Northwest 6
Life in the Northwest Coast 8
Tribes of the Southwest 10
Life in the Southwest Deserts 12
Tribes of the Midwest 14
Life in the Midwest Prairies 16
Tribes of the North 18
Life in the Northern Forests 20

Changes to a Way of Life 21
Glossary 22
Read More 23
Internet Sites 23
Critical Thinking Using the Common Core 24
Index 24

Who Were the First Americans?

Native Americans were the first Americans. Long before the United States, Canada, and Mexico were countries, Native Americans lived in North America. Many different **tribes** lived across the land. These groups of people had their own way of life. Some first Americans lived in forests, and others lived in deserts. Each tribe lived with what the land gave them.

tribe—a group of people who share the same ancestors, customs, and laws

Fact: Scientists believe the first people walked to North America. They may have crossed a land bridge from Asia to North America.

Tribes of the Northwest

Many Native American tribes lived on the Northwest **coast**. The Chinook and Haida were two of the tribes that lived in the Northwest. Tribes that lived here used the tall cedar trees to build their homes. They also made **canoes** to help them travel along the rivers. Some tribes made colorful **totem poles** from the trees.

totem pole

coast—land next to an ocean or sea

canoe—a small, shallow boat that people move through water with paddles

totem pole—a pole carved and painted with animals and other objects that represent a family

Fact: Some people in the Northwest built homes called plank houses. These homes kept them warm during cold months.

Life in the Northwest Coast

The tribes of the Northwest lived along the coast of the Pacific Ocean. Many different plants and animals also lived along the rainy coast. The people got their food from the land and water. They ate nuts and berries that grew on plants. Some tribes hunted for moose and deer in the forests. Others fished for salmon and shellfish in the ocean and rivers.

Fact: *When it was cold outside, some Northwest people wore shoes called moccasins. Clothes made from deerskin or caribou helped keep them warm.*

Tribes of the Southwest

Tribes in the Southwest lived in the hot, dry desert. Their homes kept them safe from the hot sun and wild animals. The Anasazi made homes in the side of mountains. Other tribes made **adobe** houses out of clay.

Some Southwest tribes, like the Navajo and Hopi, made baskets and jewelry. They made jewelry from silver, copper, and turquoise found in the ground.

Some Navajo still make turquoise jewelry today.

adobe—bricks made of clay and straw, dried and hardened by the heat of the sun

Anasazi homes

Life in the Southwest Deserts

There was not much rain in the Southwest. Tribes had to dig **ditches** to keep water in to help grow their plants. Some tribes, like the Navajo, were farmers. They grew corn and beans. They made food, such as soup and cornbread, with the plants they grew. Some tribes in the Southwest also hunted for animals, such as deer and antelope.

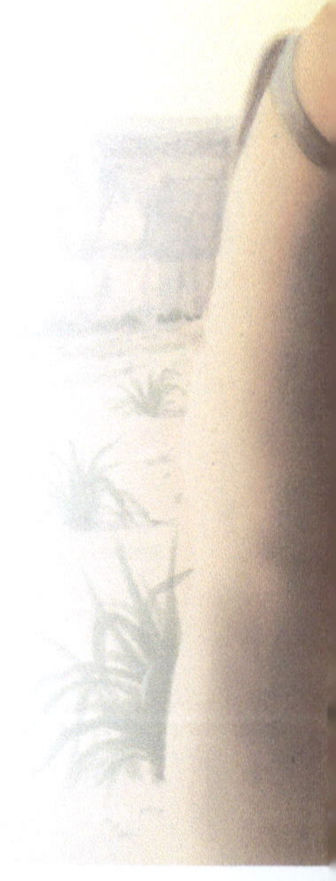

ditch—a long, narrow trench that drains water away or carries water to fields

Fact: Though many Southwest tribes were good farmers, it was a tough job without rain. Many tribes raised animals, such as sheep and goats, for meat and milk.

Tribes of the Midwest

First Americans also lived on flat, grassy **prairies** in the middle of North America. Midwest tribes are called the Plains Indians. The Dakota, the Omaha, and the different Sioux groups were some of the many Plains tribes. Some tribes lived in one place, but many Plains Indians moved a lot. They moved to follow the buffalo.

Fact: *People from different tribes did not always understand the words of other tribes. Many Plains tribes used **sign language** to talk with other tribes.*

---

prairie—a large area of flat or rolling grassland with few or no trees

sign language—hand signs that stand for words, letters, and numbers; some first Americans used Plains Indian Sign Language

Plains Indians sometimes dressed as wolves when hunting buffalo.

Life in the Midwest Prairies

The buffalo that lived on the prairie were very important to Native Americans. They were careful to only hunt the buffalo that they needed. Plains tribes hunted buffalo for food, clothes, tools, and to build their homes. Most tribes lived in **tepees** that were made of buffalo hide. When the buffalo moved, tepees could be taken down and carried to the next place.

Fact: *Besides eating buffalo, Plains tribes also ate nuts, berries, corn, and potatoes. Tribes got these foods from plants or traded with other tribes that grew them.*

tepee—cone-shaped tents made by the Plains Indians to use as homes

Tribes of the North

Long ago much of North America was covered with forests. Tribes in the North used trees from the forest to make their homes. Some tribes lived in **longhouses**. Others lived in **wigwams**. Tribes along the east coast also used the trees to make canoes. The Iroquois and the Powhatan are two of the many tribes that lived in the North.

longhouse—a long, wooden building where many families from the same Native American tribe lived together

wigwam—a hut made of poles and covered with bark or animal skins that was once a home for some Native Americans

Fact: About 60 people lived in one longhouse. Some longhouses were nearly 200 feet (61 meters) long. Wigwams were smaller. They were about 10 feet (3 meters) tall.

Life in the Northern Forests

Bears, deer, moose, and other animals lived in the forests. Beavers and many different kinds of fish lived in the rivers and lakes. The people hunted animals in the forest and caught fish in lakes for food. They also ate many plants. Some tribes, like the Iroquois, planted gardens for food. Many Iroquois lived together in **communities**.

Fact: *Some tribes ate maple syrup that they made from maple tree sap.*

community—a group of people who live in the same area

Changes to a Way of Life

The first Americans' way of life changed when people from Europe came to North America. The Europeans' way of life was much different. They spoke different languages, wore different clothes, and wanted to own the land. The two groups of people did not understand each other. As more Europeans came to America, the first Americans' way of life changed forever.

Glossary

adobe (uh-DOH-bee)—bricks made of clay and straw, dried and hardened by the heat of the sun

canoe (kuh-NOO)—a small, shallow boat that people move through water with paddles

coast (KOHST)—land next to an ocean or sea

community (kuh-MYOO-nuh-tee)—a group of people who live in the same area

ditch (DICH)—a long, narrow trench that drains water away or carries water to fields

longhouse (LAWNG-houss)—a long, wooden building where many families from the same Native American tribe lived together

prairie (PRAIR-ee)—a large area of flat or rolling grassland with few or no trees

sign language (SINE LANG-gwij)—hand signs that stand for words, letters, and numbers; Some first Americans used Plains Indian Sign Language

tepee (TEE-pee)—cone-shaped tents made by the Plains Indians to use as homes

totem pole (TOH-tuhm POHL)—a pole carved and painted with animals and other objects that represent a family

tribe (TRIBE)—a group of people who share the same ancestors, customs, and laws

wigwam (WIG-wahm)—a hut made of poles and covered with bark or animal skins that was once a home for some Native Americans

Read More

Dolbear, Emily and Benoit, Peter. *The Iroquois.* A True Book. New York: Children's Press, 2011.

Dwyer, Helen and Stout, Mary. *Hopi History and Culture.* Native American Library. New York, N.Y.: Gareth Stevens Pub., 2012.

Santella, Andrew. *Plains Indians.* First Nations of North America. Chicago: Heinemann Library, 2012.

Internet Sites

FactHound offers a safe, fun way to find Internet sites related to this book. All of the sites on FactHound have been researched by our staff.

Here's all you do:

Visit *www.facthound.com*

Type in this code: 9781515724759

Critical Thinking Using the Common Core

1. Many Plains Indians moved often to follow the buffalo. Why do you think tribes in the North chose to stay in the same place? (Integration of Knowledge and Ideas)
2. Tribes across the land lived in different types of homes. Which type of home would you like to have lived in? Explain why. (Integration of Knowledge and Ideas.)

Index

canoe, 6, 18
clothes, 8, 16, 21
  moccasins, 8
Europeans, 21
first Americans, 4, 5
  Midwest, 14, 16
  North, 18, 19, 20
  Northwest, 6, 7, 8
  Southwest, 10, 12, 13
food, 8, 12, 13, 16, 20
homes, 6, 7, 10, 11, 16, 18, 19
  adobe, 10
  longhouse, 18, 19
  plank house, 7
  tepee, 16
  wigwam, 18, 19
hunting, 8, 12, 15, 16, 20
language, 14, 21
planting, 12, 13, 20